CRICKET
SKILLS

FOR AUSSIE KIDS

GARRY POWELL

Wellington
books for kids

Cricket Skills for Aussie Kids

ISBN: 978-1-925308-97-6 (paperback)
ISBN:978-1-925308-98-3 (digital online)

Wellington (Aust.) Pty Ltd
ABN 30 062 365 413
433 Wellington Street
Clifton Hill
VIC 3068

Love this book?
Visit kidzbookhub.com online to find more great titles.

CONTENTS

INTRODUCTION

Cricket is a bat and ball game.

At competition level the teams must have equal numbers.

For traditional cricket it is 11 players in each team. Indoor and limited-over cricket can have 5–8 per team. The two teams take it in turn to bat and field.

The fielding team tries to get the batting team out while the batting team tries to score runs. Runs are scored when batters hit the ball away from fielders and run the length of the pitch, or when the ball travels over a marked boundary line.

The aim of the game is to score more runs than the other team.

Older players use a hard ball and lots of added equipment. Juniors often play with a soft ball so that not much equipment is needed.

This book has been written with right-handed cricketers in mind. Left handers will have to reverse the instructions. For example an off spin moves away from the hand that delivers it. In the case of a right hander this would be to the right. In the case of a left hander to the left.

A group playing cricket, the batsman by the wicket at left ready to hit the ball, a young boy sitting in the right foreground taking score; after an untraced painting by Hayman for Vauxhall Gardens (Allen CL 214). 1743

HISTORY

The origin for the name of the game of cricket is unclear. The word 'criquet' in French means goal post or stick.

Today, the strong cricket playing nations all spring from England and its former colonies: England, India, Pakistan, Sri Lanka, Australia, New Zealand, South Africa, West Indies and Canada. The commonly accepted name of the game we know as cricket is from the English words 'cricce', which means staff and 'wicket', which means wooden gate.

In the Middle Ages in England, shepherds and monks played a game where they used their staffs to protect a gate wicket from a round object bowled underarm.

Certainly, cricket was popular as a recreation in England during this time, and by the 1700s became the game we know.

IMPORTANT DATES

1700   Cricket matches played regularly in England

1721   First recorded cricket match in India

1739   First first-class match held in England

1838   Melbourne Cricket Club formed

1848   Bombay Cricket Club formed

1850   Australia's first interstate match:
Victoria v. Tasmania

1864   India's first first-class match: Madras v. Calcutta

1877   First test match was between Australia and
England at the Melbourne Cricket Ground

1932   India's first Test match was against England at
Lords Cricket Ground

1948   Don Bradman's 'Invincibles' team toured England
and remained undefeated

1971   First one-day limited-over match:
Australia v. England at the MCG

1975 First cricket world cup was played in England and
      won by West Indies

2005 First international 20/20 match played by
      Australia v. New Zealand

2008 India's Premier League formed

Charterhouse Hospital, London:
boys playing cricket. 1804.

OVERARM BOWLING

There are four parts to bowling: the grip, the run-up, the delivery and the follow-through.

Grip

→   The ball is held more in the fingers than in the palm of the hand.

→   The positioning of the fingers depends on the intended bowling type: fast, swing, off-spin, leg-spin.

→   The basic grip is to hold the ball so the seam is vertical, the middle finger on one side of the seam and the index finger on the other side. The thumb should be under the ball and straight along the seam.

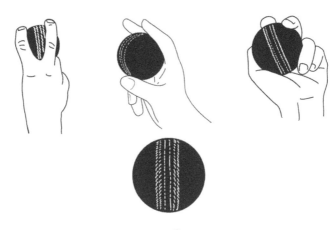

Run-up

→ This can include 5–11 steps, and is a smooth run rather than fast.

→ Start with slower strides and gather pace to reach the fastest step to occur at the delivery stride.

→ The bowler's eyes should be looking at the proposed landing spot of the ball.

Delivery

→ At the bowling crease there is a jump into the delivery stride and the body should be leaning a little away from the target.

→ The ball is held with a bent arm and near to the chin, the free arm reaching high.

→ The landing from the jump is on the foot opposite to the bowling arm. This foot is then anchored to the ground and the bowling arm swings through straight and high to release the ball.

Follow-through

→ The bowling arm comes down and across the body after the ball is released.

→ The other arm swings backwards as a counter balance.

→ Slowing strides lead the body down the line of the bowl and then the bowler off to the side of the pitch.

BATTING

There are four parts to batting: the grip, the stance, the back lift and the shot (stroke).

Grip

→   The hands are held close together in the middle of the handle. This lets them work together at the same time. The right hand (dominant hand) is at the back and below the left hand which is above on the front.

→   The V shape formed by the thumbs and the fingers point down to the back of the bat. This means the back of the top hand and the palm of the bottom hand point towards the bowler.

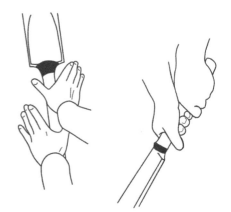

Stance

→ The ready position is standing tall, side on to the bowler.

→ The body should be relaxed, knees slightly bent, one foot either side of the batting crease.

→ The batter's eyes should be level to the ground, left shoulder pointing at the bowler and knees slightly bent.

→ The bat should rest lightly on the ground near the back foot.

→ Body weight should be spread equally onto both feet.

Back lift

→ The bat should be lifted straight back towards the middle stump.

→ The top hand pushes it back more than the bottom hand pulling it.

Shots

Front-foot shots

→ These are made when the ball lands close to the batter.

→ After the backlift the first thing that moves is the front foot. This move places the front foot near to where the ball lands.

→ *Forward defence*

- Used to protect the wicket by stopping the ball from hitting the stumps.
- The ball is watched right onto the bat.
- Back lift, then forward lean — leading with the head and left shoulder, with forward step in line with the ball.
- The bat is brought forward alongside the front pad so that there is almost no gap between bat and pad.
- The left elbow (front one) is kept high so that when the ball hits the bat this is directly under the batter's head. Letting the ball hit the bat rather than the bat hit the ball makes sure that the ball drops straight down onto the pitch.

→ *Forward attack*

- Unlike the defence shot, in the attack the bat hits the ball, which gives it speed away from the bat.
- This shot is played when the ball reaches the bat without bouncing (full toss) or when it lands close to the batter (half volley).
- The foot placement is similar to the forward defence, but the backlift is higher and the bat doesn't stop near the front pad.

- After hitting the ball, the bat follows through in the intended path of the hit ball.

- This step — back lift — forward swing — hit — follow-through — can hit the ball a long way.

Back-foot shots

→ These are played when the ball lands well short of the batter and bounces to about waist high.

→ As with front-foot shots, the first thing to move after the backlift is a foot. But this time it is the back foot and it steps back.

→ *Backwards defence*

- The ball must be watched right onto the bat and this time it is watched over the batters front shoulder.

- The top hand does most of the lifting.

- The back foot steps backwards and across in line with the off-stump. Then the front foot moves back to join it.

- The front elbow is high, firm grip of the bat with the top hand, but a relaxed bottom hand brings the bat to vertical and in line with the ball.
- Being a defensive shot, the ball hits the bat.

→ *Back-foot attack:*

- If the line of a short ball is just outside the off-stump, an attacking back-foot shot (drive or punch shot) can be played.
- The preparation is similar to the back-foot defence, but the bat swings through to hit the ball rather than letting the ball hit the bat.

FIELDING

There are three key skills in fielding: the stop, the catch and the throw.

The stop

→ An important skill needed by a fielder is to stop a hit ball as quickly as possible and return it to an end of the pitch to prevent the batter scoring runs.

→ For a ground ball: the fielder watches the ball and moves into its oncoming path. Have cupped hands so that the fingers point down. Then the ball is allowed to come into the hands. If possible and time permits the body is put behind the hands to block the oncoming ball if the hands are missed.

The catch

→ If a fielder catches a hit ball, this puts the batter out.

→ The fielder moves into the path of the oncoming ball. Arms are held comfortably in front to allow them to 'give' in order to soften the landing of the ball into the hands. The ball is watched right into the hands.

→ To catch a ball above the waist, fingers point up with thumbs together.

→ To catch below the waist, fingers point slightly down with little fingers together.

The throw

→ After fielding the ball, it is returned to the wicketkeeper — underarm if close by, or overarm from a distance.

→ The ball is held in the fingers and not the palm of the hand.

→ The body turns sideways to the target in preparation.

→ With the throwing arm, the ball is brought back behind the ear — elbow relaxed and arm slightly bent.

→ The back foot pushes off and a step is taken by the front foot towards the target.

→ At the same time, the elbow of the throwing arm leads the whole arm quickly forward.

→ The ball is released as the hand passes over the elbow.

→ The throwing arm and shoulder follow-through towards the target.

HARDER SKILLS

The game of cricket requires a variety of skills.

Bowling

→ After the basics of overarm bowling are learned and the ball can usually land on a good length so it will hit the stumps, then more advanced types of bowling can be tried.

- *Swing:* By holding it in special ways the cricket ball can be made to swerve either left or right in the air.

- *Seam:* By landing a ball on its seam it can be made to veer off the pitch either left or right.

- *Off-spin (right hand):* By holding the ball in a special way and using the fingers to spin the ball from right to left, this in turn can make the ball turn off the pitch to the right.

- *Leg-spin:* Spinning the ball by hand so that it turns off the pitch to the bowler's left.

Wicketkeeping

→ This is specialised fielding, with extra equipment needed.

Batting

→ **Hits to square of the wicket:** Leg side — pull and hook, off-side — square cut.

→ **Hits to behind the wicket:** Leg side — leg glance, off-side — late cut.

→ **Hits to in front of the wicket:** On drive (leg side), straight drive, off drive and cover drive (off-side).

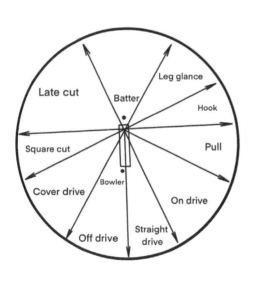

Direction of shots

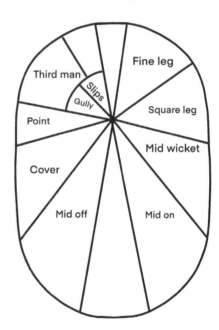

Field positions

PRACTISING BY YOURSELF

Bowling

→ A brick, concrete or other hard surface wall is needed to bowl against.

→ A soft ball (e.g. tennis ball) is best to use for most practice, as it bounces and you don't have to chase it very far. Also a hard ball can damage a wall and in turn be damaged by the wall.

→ To use a real cricket ball a rebound net is needed.

→ Bowl from a standing position (i.e. without a run-up) and make the ball bounce only once before hitting the wall.

→ Rock and bowl — rock your weight from your back foot onto your front foot three times. On the third rock bowl the ball. Your arms rock at the same time: 130–180 degrees.

→ Bowl from one step. Then bowl from three steps and finally from a full run-up. Always the ball should bounce just once before hitting the wall.

→ Bowl to hit a set of stumps marked on a wall.

→ Bowl so that the ball lands on a target before hitting the wall.

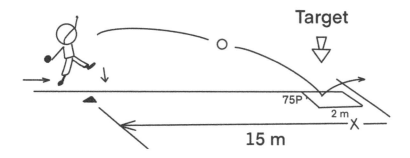

→ Score target hits

- From standing, one step, a 3-step run-up, 5-step run-up, 7-step run-up.
- Work out which is easier and how to get the best score.

→ To increase difficulty

- Decrease the size of the target.
- Increase the distance the ball has to travel.
- Increase or decrease the speed of the ball from what is comfortable.

→ To decrease difficulty

- remove a target altogether and just bowl against a wall or rebound net.

→ The same practices can be used for:

- Simple overarm bowling
- Fast bowling
- Off-spin bowling leg-spin bowling.

Batting

First use a soft ball (like a tennis ball), then a hard ball when your skill improves.

→ Hit a ball from a batting tee.

- It is best to use a tee that can be changed up and down so that you can alter the height of the ball and so practice different shots.

- When the ball is low you can practice your front-foot shots — on the lowest you can step forward and drive the ball straight.

- For the sweep shot you can step forward and swing the bat almost horizontally so the ball travels sideways.

→ Hit the ball towards a target.

→ Hang an old ball in a stocking. Now you can practise both front-foot and back-foot shots.

→ See how many times in a row you can hit the ball.

→ Throw a ball against a wall and hit the rebound.

→ Hit the ball against a wall and again on the rebound.

→ See how many times in a row you can hit the ball against a wall.

Fielding — throwing

This is for underarm throws that would be close to the wicket and overarm throws from a further distance.

Use a tennis ball because it rebounds back from a brick/stone wall really well.

→ Throw against a wall, trying to remember good technique, both underarm and overarm.

→ Throw hard and fast so that it rebounds faster and further.

→ Throw the ball so that it travels slowly to the wall and just reaches it, so as to only rebound a little.

→ Increase the distance you throw the ball.

→ Throw while sitting.

→ Draw different targets on a wall and try to hit them.

→ Score direct hits out of 10 throws — vary the distance.

→ Run and pick up a ball that is still on the ground — throw it at a wall for accuracy and distance.

→ Use actual cricket stumps as a target.

→ Especially underarm, practise throwing both left and right hands, as this throw is usually a short and quick one in a match situation.

Fielding — stopping

→ Roll a ball along the ground, and run and pick it up.

→ Roll a ball against a wall and stop the rebound.

→ Underarm throw against a wall and stop the rebound.

→ Overarm throw against a wall and stop the rebound.

→ Use all of these stops, with a following throw at a target on the wall.

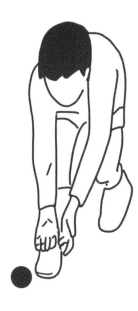

Fielding — catching

→ Throw a ball into the air and catch it.

→ Throw a ball high underarm and run to catch it.

→ Throw a ball overarm and run to catch it.

→ Throw against a wall, both underarm and overarm and catch the return.

→ Try to catch 10 in a row, then 20 in a row.

→ Change the height, distance and speed of the throw and catch.

→ Throw and catch while sitting.

→ Throw and catch one hand only, then change hands.

High   Chest high   Low   Chest high to the side

PRACTISING WITH A PARTNER

Bowling

→ This practice/play is the most flexible of all because:
- both can be bowlers and bowl to each other
- one can be a bowler and one a fielder/ wicketkeeper
- one a bowler and one a batter (with a wall as a backstop).

→ If both are bowlers, you can bowl to each other or both bowl from the same end against a wall.

→ Follow the leader: change the run-up, style (e.g. fast or spin) or landing area (full or short).

→ 10 up — bowling and batting in turn — the first to hit a target 10 times.

→ Bowler to keeper — see how many catches you can get in a row.

→ Bowler to batter — see how many 'outs' by the bowler and how many hits along the ground by the batter.

→ **Line and length bowling**
  ◆ Mark out a 'good length' area on the ground in the line of the off-stump.
  ◆ Practise all styles of bowling using different line and length.

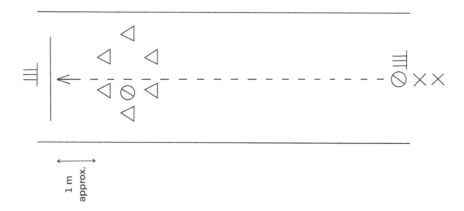

Batting

→ From a golf tee, the batter tries to hit the ball direct to where ever their fielding partner is. Take turns to be batter.

→ Hit a ball rolled to you by the fielder/partner.

→ Hit balls thrown underarm to you.

→ Hit balls thrown to you (throw-downs) overarm.

→ Hit balls bowled to you — practise different shots by changing the landing positions of the bowls or throws.

→ The right shot — target area for the feeder (thrower or bowler) is changed after a set number of balls (e.g. 10 throws landing close to the batter that require a front-foot shot, then 10 throws short that require a back-foot shot).

→ Target hit — the batter has to hit a fed ball to a target (e.g. a side wall).

→ Mini test match — using real stumps or ones painted onto a suitable surface.

  • The bowler bowls 4×6-ball overs. The batter tries to score imaginary runs, such as: if a ball is defended = no run, if hit slowly away from the wicket = one run, if hit to a designated boundary (e.g. side wall, fence or gutter = four runs).

- The batter is 'out' if the ball hits the stumps, if the ball is snicked/deflected behind the stumps, or if the ball passes over the boundary 'on the full'.

Wall

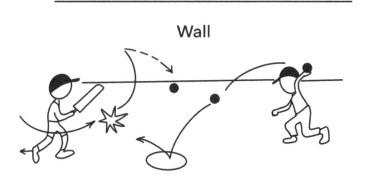

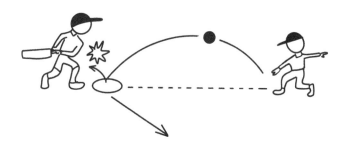

Fielding

→ Take turns to be the thrower and the fielder/stopper/ catcher.

→ Roll, throw or bowl balls to a partner. Change the distance of the throw, the speed, the angle and height of the ball flight.

→ 10 up — a competition to throw a ball at a target — first to 10 hits wins the contest.

→ Hit balls to a partner.

Blockers (4-6 players)

→ Two teams of two or three players face each other about 15-25 metres apart.

→ Just behind each team is a goal line. Each team tries to roll or underarm the ball across the other's line.

Classic soft catches (4–6 players)

→ To be played in an area about 6 metres wide and 12 metres long. If ground markings exist, use them (e.g. a badminton court, a bat tennis court or a third of a netball court).

→ String a rope across the middle 3 metres high to act as a net. Two or three players on each side of the net.

→ A ball is thrown underarm over the rope or net and the other team try to catch it. If they catch the ball they score a point. If the ball hits the ground they lose a point.

→ Take turns to throw — first to 10 points is the winner.

→ If only two players, the playing area should only be about 4 × 8 metres.

Zone catches

→ A variation of classic catches is zone catches.

→ Each team has a 'home zone' of about 10 × 10 metres and these zones are about 20 metres apart.

→ The ball has to be thrown overarm to cross the neutral area and land in the opposition's area.

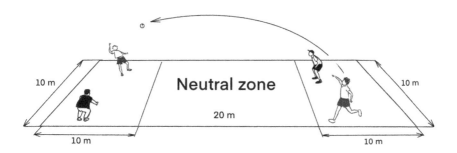

Tippity-run (4–8 players)

→ There are two teams of equal numbers — one team batting and one team bowling.

→ When batting, each team faces a minimum of 24 balls, and each member of the bowling team must bowl a minimum of six balls.

→ Two batters face two overs between them.

→ The batter taking strike for the first ball of each over must be different.

→ Then the next two batters face two overs, and so on.

→ If the batter hits the ball with the bat, no matter where the ball goes they must run, even if it is merely tipped/snicked.

→ Runs can only be scored by the batters running between the wickets.

→ Batters can be out by being bowled, caught, stumped or run out.

→ When 'out' the batter stays batting, but the fielding team scores four runs for the dismissal.

→ There can be double and even triple plays: both batters run out, catch and run-outs.

French cricket (4–8 players)

→ One player is the batter and all the rest are fielders.

→ Using underarm throws with a tennis ball, the fielders try to hit the batter's legs below the knees.

→ The batter must not move their feet at all (as if they are glued to the ground). However, they can twist and turn their body and arms as much as they like. This means that whatever the direction the throw comes from, they can protect their legs with the bat.

→ The fielder of the ball has two choices. They can throw at the batter's legs from where they field the ball, or pass it to another fielder in a better position. If the passed ball is caught it Gan be thrown at the batter's legs. If it is not caught, then it must be passed again.

→ The batter is out if the ball hits their legs or a hit ball is caught.

→ The fielder who gets the batter out becomes the new batter. If they have already been the batter, they may choose a substitute batter who has not had a turn.

→ If the batter is not out after 20 hits they must retire. Then they choose a player who hasn't had a turn to take their place as the batter.

Continuous cricket (8+ players)

→ The group is divided into two teams.

→ The fielding team has one bowler and one wicketkeeper, and the rest are fielders. Using a tennis ball, the bowler bowls underarm so the ball bounces only once before it reaches the batter.

→ If the batter hits the ball they must run around a marker about 7 metres to the side of the pitch and get back to their batting position as soon as possible.

→ The fielders have to get the ball back to the bowler as soon as possible — because as soon as the bowler has the ball in their marked area, they can bowl at the stumps whether the batter is there or not.

→ A batter is out if the ball hits the wicket or a hit ball is caught.

→ When one batter is out, the next batter has to 'face up' immediately. This is again because the bowler can bowl at the wicket whether a batter is in position or not.

→ A run is scored each time a batter rounds the side marker. Sides change over when all the batters are out.

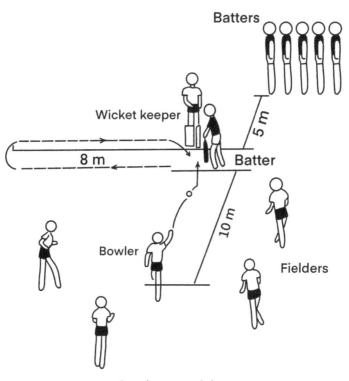

Batters

Wicket keeper

5 m

8 m

Batter

10 m

Bowler

Fielders

Continuous cricket

One-hit cricket (4–8 players)

→ There is one batter and one bowler, and the rest are fielders.

→ The bowler bowls to the batter, who after they hit the ball stands off to the side of the pitch instead of running anywhere.

→ The player who fields the ball throws at the stumps from where they stop it. If the ball hits the stumps, the batter is out and the fielder replaces the batter.

→ If the ball misses the stumps it is returned to the bowler and another ball is bowled.

→ The batter is out if the ball hits the stumps either by a bowl or by a fielder's return, or if a hit ball is caught.

→ After one over of six balls, there is a new bowler. Bowlers change until all players have had a turn.

→ If the batter is not out after three overs (18 balls), they retire to be replaced by another batter.

Line cricket (4–8 players)

→ For this game, lines need to be drawn or markers put down.

→ Players take it in turns to be batter, bowler and fielder.

→ Batters each face an equal number of balls — 6 or 12.

→ Runs are scored by the distance the ball is hit: over the first line scores one run, two runs over the second, three over the third, and so on.

→ There are no wickets, but even if the batter is caught out they remain as batter until they face their required number of balls.

→ If the batter is caught out, four runs are taken from their total score.

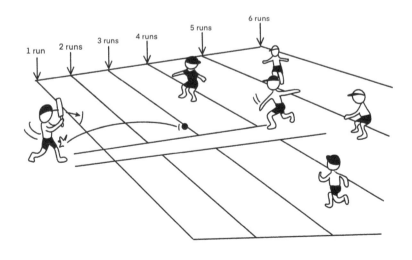

Three-sixty rotation (5–10 players)

→ Players rotate through the total number of positions.

→ Five players: bowler, batter, wicketkeeper, off-side fielder, on-side fielder.

→ Ten players: as the numbers increase the players/ fielder can number up to seven.

→ After each over every player moves around one place.

→ The batter doesn't run after hitting the ball. Runs are scored as follows: one run if the batter hits the ball, two runs if the ball goes past the fielders, and four runs if it reaches the boundary markers.

→ Runs can only be scored in front of the wicket.

→ Even if the batter is dismissed, they stay as batter for their allocated number of balls (usually one over).

Kanga couples (8–12 players)

→ The game is played in pairs (teams of two).

→ Before the game, each pair is given a number: 1–6.

→ Each pair takes it in turns to be bowlers, batters, fielders. A starting example for 10 players (five pairs) might be: pair 1 — bowlers, pair 2 — batters, couples 3-4-5 — fielders.

→ Runs can only be scored by the batters running between the wickets.

Kanga cricket (16–24 players — two teams of 8–12)

→ Teams bat and field for half the game each.

→ The 'next pair in' for the batting team are the umpires, while all others in the batting team wait beyond the boundary. This cuts change-over time between batting pairs.

→ Each pair face the same number of balls no matter how many times they are given out.

→ Every player bowls an equal number of balls (e.g. one over of six balls).

→ There is no leg before wicket (LBW).

→ Each time a batter is out, the next ball must be faced by their partner.

→ A team's score is established by dividing the total number of runs by the number of times they are out.

WARM UP AND WARM DOWN

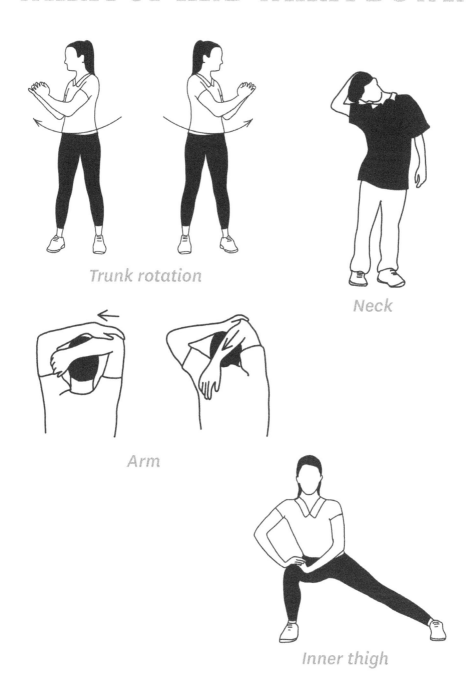

Trunk rotation

Neck

Arm

Inner thigh

Thigh

Calf

Hamstring

Lower back

CRICKET TALK

appeal — if a fielder believes a batter is out, they yell 'How's that?' as a request for the umpire to make a decision.

back-foot shot — a shot played when the batter steps back towards the stumps from their 'stance' position.

back lift — the raising of the bat before a shot is played.

bails — the two round tube-like woods that sit on the stumps to form the wicket.

ball — the count when the ball is bowled to the batter.

bat — the instrument the batter uses to protect the wicket and hit the oncoming ball.

batters — players protecting the wicket and trying to score runs.

block — the line of sight between the two wickets at either end of the pitch.

bye — a run taken even when the batter doesn't hit the ball.

crease — there are three lines marked at each end of the pitch: popping crease, bowling crease and return crease.

cut — a shot to the off-side with a mostly horizontal bat.

drive — an attacking shot taking the ball in front of the wicket.

extra — a run scored without necessarily hitting the ball.

fielding positions — positions where the fielders stand.

front-foot shot — a shot where the batter steps forward to hit the ball.

four — runs scored when the ball is hit to the boundary line.

full toss — a ball bowled so that it doesn't bounce before reaching the batter.

half volley — a bowl that lands just in front of the batter.

hat trick — when a bowler gets three batters out in successive balls.

innings — a team's turn to bat or a batter's time at bat.

no-ball — an illegal ball bowled.

off-side — the half of the field to the right of a right-handed batter.

on-side — the half of the field to the left of a right-handed batter.

over the wicket — when the bowler's delivery arm is closest to the stumps.

six — runs scored when the ball is hit over the boundary line 'on the full'.

stumps — the three wooden sticks that form the base of the wicket.

umpire — the referee in charge of the game.

wide — a bowled ball that is too wide for the batter to hit.

yorker — a bowl that lands at the batter's toes.